GW01314784

Illustrations by Danny Burgess

Layout Design by Olivia Wright

CONTENTS

ABOUT THE AUTHORS

Hi, we're Liz and Matt and we are professional communicators with over 30 years of experience between us, and a list of satisfied clients who ask us back again and again to work with their teams.

We have run meetings and workshops and given speeches for thousands of groups, across audiences of all sizes, nationalities and industries, We're practitioners, not professors, who've learned by doing. This stuff is our craft and our passion and we're sharing the tricks of our trade to help others succeed in theirs.

Our principles are based in neuroscience, and our structure-in-disguise approach makes working with us fun and experiential, so the learning lasts.

We have lots of friends who are very important and influential in the business world but we refuse to tap any of them up for a meaningless quote about how great they think this book is. You'll just have to read it and make up your own mind.

OUR CRUSADE
The reason behind this book

We could never have predicted, as an introvert and a person with stage fright, that our career paths would take us towards becoming professional communicators. This journey has proven to us that no human being needs to have "presentation skills training". You go to a shop and interact with the staff, you sit at dinner with family and friends and chat. You are therefore capable of communicating effectively.

The books that tell you how not to be frightened about presenting are holding you back. We won't be doing any of that. We'll be helping you work out the presentation superpowers you already possess and which you want to develop – and showing you how to develop them.

We're not promising you a change of persona (you're great as you are!), we won't stop shy people being shy, and we don't want you to be any different – just your best shiny self.

What we've found most useful is to take the weight of expectation away from the established 'business presentation' format. We spend so much time in meetings at work; surely this time deserves to be effective. This book will help you move from meeting to workshop and from one-way communication to two-way interaction, with you as the navigator who gets people where they need to be.

That's why this is not your usual presentation skills book

NOT YOUR USUAL

STOP!

Read this first (disclaimers)

There are no clever diagrams or theoretical models in this book. If you are expecting such things, put it down and walk away.

All you'll get is some real-world thinking and tips, brought to life with great illustrations from our friend and fellow expert, Danny.

We can't put down in here everything we know – even we would be bored reading that all in one go – so we've gone for a collection of stuff that will get you off to a good start. If we get enough positive feedback, we'll write volume 2, 3, 4 and the rest.

Obviously, anyone who reads this book has their own context, and not everything we suggest will be appropriate or useful. Take it as it comes, it's intended to help, just pick the bits that work for you and ignore the rest – we don't want to get anyone in trouble.

We've got used to talking about things in certain ways and expressing ourselves through a set of analogies and language. It's not gospel and it's not patented or rights-managed, so if you don't like it, change it and if you love it, steal it.

We're not writers! We are better in person, on our feet. We don't like the concept of editing so have kept our content raw – like it would be when we speak it aloud. Apologies for any massacring of the English Language.

Are you a bit messy?

Want to start again?

Or just reading online!

Worksheets can be downloaded at:
www.thebusinessspeakeasy.com/NYUbook

TO GET THE MOST FROM THIS BOOK YOU WILL NEED...

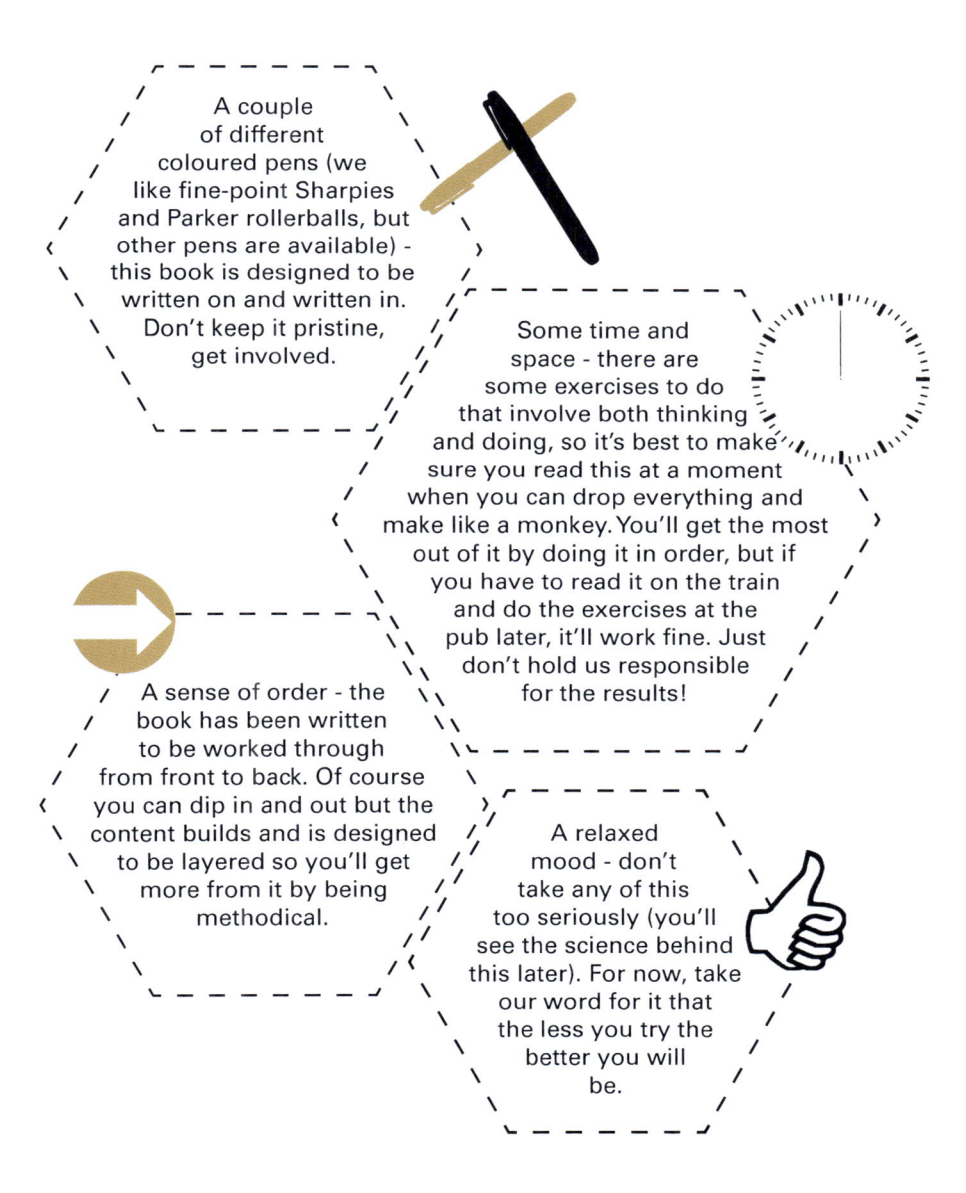

A couple of different coloured pens (we like fine-point Sharpies and Parker rollerballs, but other pens are available) - this book is designed to be written on and written in. Don't keep it pristine, get involved.

Some time and space - there are some exercises to do that involve both thinking and doing, so it's best to make sure you read this at a moment when you can drop everything and make like a monkey. You'll get the most out of it by doing it in order, but if you have to read it on the train and do the exercises at the pub later, it'll work fine. Just don't hold us responsible for the results!

A sense of order - the book has been written to be worked through from front to back. Of course you can dip in and out but the content builds and is designed to be layered so you'll get more from it by being methodical.

A relaxed mood - don't take any of this too seriously (you'll see the science behind this later). For now, take our word for it that the less you try the better you will be.

SO WHAT IS THIS BOOK ABOUT THEN, IF IT'S NOT PRESENTATIONS?

This book is about what are traditionally called "presentations". It's also about chats, meetings, conferences, workshops, discussions – in fact, any interaction between 2 or more people.

However, all this language puts us into a pattern of thinking that's often unhelpful. For any of these interactions we prefer to think about **getting people where they need to be**.

When we mention any of these things in the course of the book, this is what we mean by it...

STOP THINKING LIKE THIS...

Presentation

A process of sharing a topic with an audience. Typically a demonstration or speech with the intention of informing, persuading or building goodwill.

Speech

A formal address or discourse delivered to an audience.

Workshop

A meeting at which a group of people engage in intensive discussion or activity on a particular subject or project.

Meeting

A gathering of 2 or more people that has been convened for the purpose of achieving a common goal through verbal interaction, such as sharing information or reaching agreement.

START THINKING LIKE THIS...

A session that gets people where they need to be with regards to the topic at hand.

-1-
INTRODUCTION

BEING vs. DOING

There's a whole lot to this presentations business, and it can be a bit daunting to get your head around all of it at once. We've been learning for years and we still don't know everything there is to know. But we do know quite a lot!

The biggest thing we've learned is that most people focus on the "doing' of presentations: content, slides, scripts, how to introduce yourself and all that jazz. However, that's not the part that can unlock brilliance. Nor is it the part that will stop you having presentation nerves, keep you from getting tripped up along the way and losing your train of thought, or help you stay strong in the face of tricky questions or awkward attendees.

While the Doing stuff is of course important, there's another side to presentation brilliance.

THE 4 AREAS OF GREAT COMMUNICATION

BEING

Communication superpowers:

Gain confidence in your own authentic style.

Have more presence and impact in a room.

Energy, flow and range:

Create the right energy in your audience/participants.

Learn tactics to keep you and your presentation on track.

DOING

Handling your audience:

Get audiences engaged from the start.

Manage tricky customers with ease.

Bringing content to life:

Breathe life into content (even PowerPoint!)

Tell compelling stories using a simple structure.

AND ANOTHER THING...

As you can probably tell, we fundamentally disagree with a lot of the received wisdom about giving presentations. It makes us quite cross actually.

But there's no smoke without fire, and most of these myths have grown in order to help people get around real life issues and potential pitfalls,

Our intention in this book is to expose some of the myths, and examine the real facts behind them, while giving you useful stuff you can do to help yourself too.

2

COMMUNICATION
SUPERPOWERS

MY SUPERPOWERS

MYTH: Smooth and slick presentations are the gold standard we should all aim for.

FACT: A little bit of sick comes into our mouths when we hear about the methods used to 'increase impact'. Pausing artificially for impact reduces your impact. Strategic hand gestures make you look like a TV weather presenter. Feeling comfortable will enable you to create maximum impact.

MYTH: There's you the normal person, and then there's a separate you that's a 'presenter'.

FACT: Nothing turns off participants more than seeing someone they know well, or would like to know well, being someone they're not. Being yourself, talking the way you do at the pub or round the breakfast table on a weekend; that's you at your most entertaining and effective.

Books are great, but they're normally one-way traffic in terms of communication. Let's get into some engaging, two-way stuff and find out what raw materials you've got to work with. That way, this book will help you move from useful thoughts into useful actions.

Everyone brings something to the party when it comes to communication. If you have voices in your head telling you you've nothing to offer, they are lying. If you struggle to think of anything during the next exercise, then ask a good friend or mentor to help you think about it and give you some stimulus.

TRY THIS ...

My Communication Superpowers

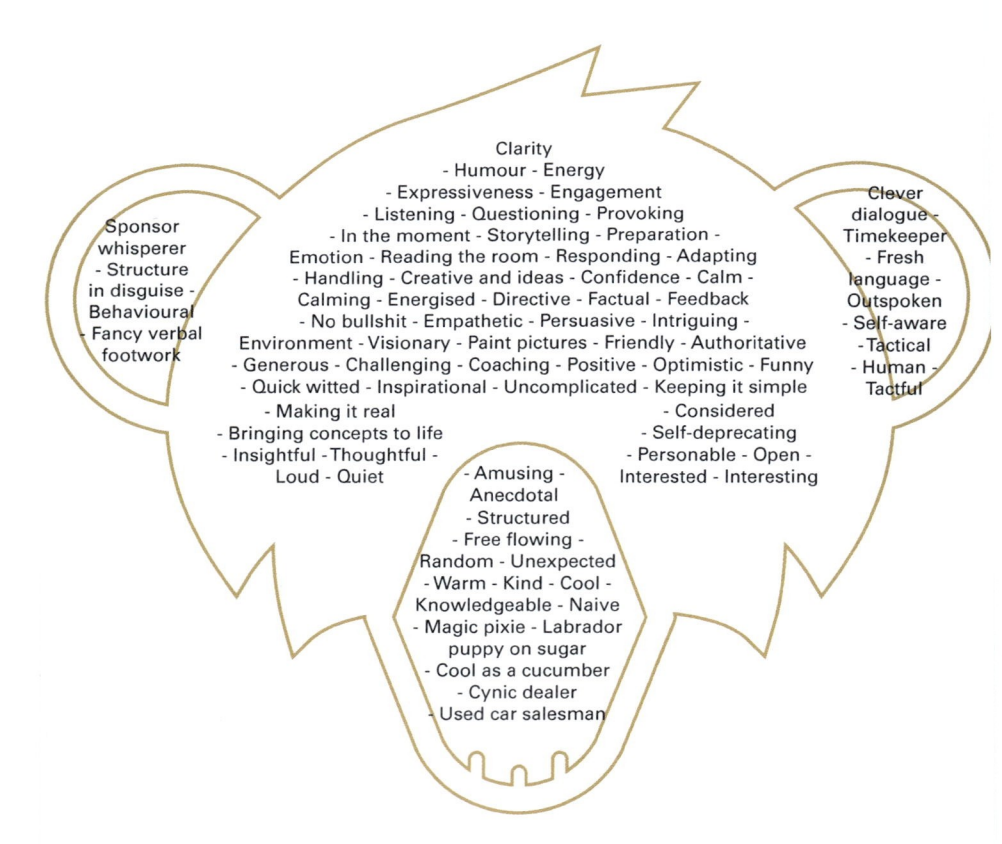

Use this sheet to list the Superpowers you have, and those you want. The words in the monkey head are there to help you - but feel free to go off-piste... it's your list!

Sponsor whisperer - Structure in disguise - Behavioural - Fancy verbal footwork

Clarity
- Humour - Energy
- Expressiveness - Engagement
- Listening - Questioning - Provoking
- In the moment - Storytelling - Preparation -
Emotion - Reading the room - Responding - Adapting
- Handling - Creative and ideas - Confidence - Calm -
Calming - Energised - Directive - Factual - Feedback
- No bullshit - Empathetic - Persuasive - Intriguing -
Environment - Visionary - Paint pictures - Friendly - Authoritative
- Generous - Challenging - Coaching - Positive - Optimistic - Funny
- Quick witted - Inspirational - Uncomplicated - Keeping it simple
- Making it real
- Bringing concepts to life
- Insightful - Thoughtful -
Loud - Quiet

Clever dialogue - Timekeeper - Fresh language - Outspoken - Self-aware - Tactical - Human - Tactful

- Considered
- Self-deprecating -
Personable - Open -
Interested - Interesting

- Amusing -
Anecdotal
- Structured
- Free flowing -
Random - Unexpected
- Warm - Kind - Cool -
Knowledgeable - Naive
- Magic pixie - Labrador
puppy on sugar
- Cool as a cucumber
- Cynic dealer
- Used car salesman

SUPERPOWERS I'VE GOT...

SUPERPOWERS I WANT...

This page can now act as a reference for you. It's useful to tune in to what you're great at so you can amplify it, and also it will help you have a clear view of what you're going for when reading and using this book.

SUPERPOWER *(noun)* – the skills or abilities you have which make you the amazing individual you are when it comes to a particular topic. Specifically here...

The ones you've got: the things you're good at when leading in a room with other people.

The ones you want: not necessarily stuff you're bad at, rather things you think that, if amplified, would make you even more effective.

ENERGY, RANGE AND FLOW

THE BRAIN
How yours (and everyone else's) works best

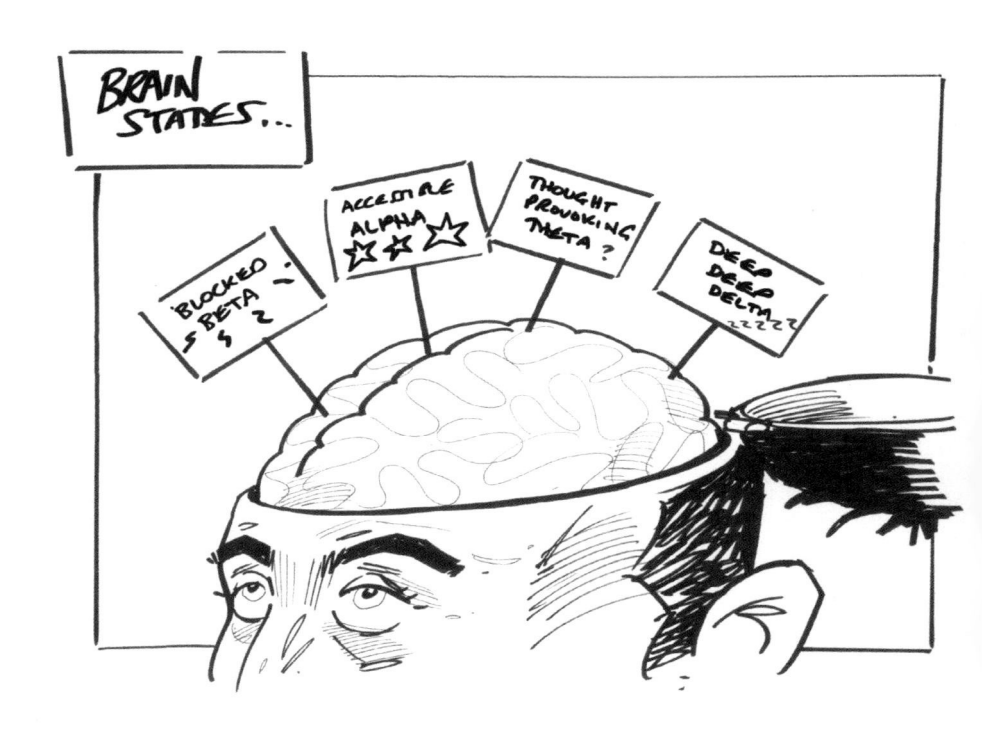

Although we communicate with our mouths and bodies, what's really going on is the passing of information between brains: a fact we often forget in business. The state of your brain dictates your ability to communicate effectively and the state of other people's brains dictates their ability to collaborate with you.

When our brain isn't in the right place, we stutter, falter, get nervous and later get annoyed that we didn't make the most of a situation. In the right place - that great place that athletes call 'flow' - we can always be our best and get the best from every interaction.

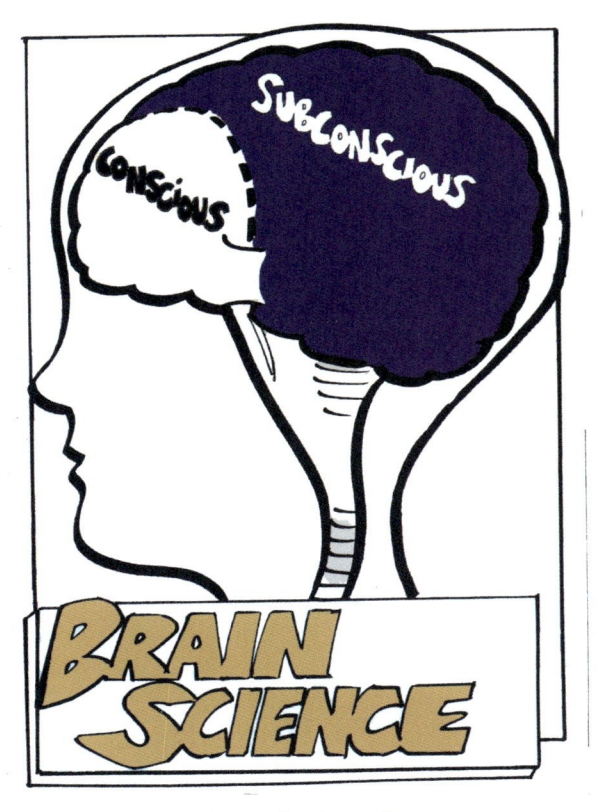

First, some simple brain science – or, at least, the way we see it based on the clever stuff we've read and the experiences we've had.

We like to think about the brain in terms of the conscious and subconscious mind. They're less a physical area of your brain and more two distinct types of processing power.

Conscious processing

The conscious is the bit that is talking to you as you read this book. It's powerful and it gets stuff done. In a life or death situation, your conscious brain will take over and create action or fear response. In daily work, your conscious is busy trying to concentrate on all the things you need to be doing right now.

Trouble is, the conscious brain can handle on average only seven bits of data. That means that most of us can actively focus on a total of seven simple things. Try holding a 9-digit number sequence in your head, and see how that goes for you. The seven things are constantly changing - the truth is nobody can multi-task, we can merely switch more or less quickly between those seven things. The conscious brain is energy hungry and using it on its own for long periods is draining for human beings.

Subconscious processing

The subconscious, on the other hand, is where the magic happens. Like an infinite Gb device, it is noting, recording and processing everything you experience (including a lot of stuff you haven't even consciously noticed).

This means it contains a wealth of stored stimulus, and is the treasure trove in which your brain can make new connections and have ideas, and appreciate different points of view.

> **MYTH:** Serious subjects need dry, businesslike treatment.
>
> **FACT:** Whatever the subject matter, taking a relaxed (but not inappropriately irreverent) approach will help brains focus on and work with key messages. The human brain is more effective when the human being it's sitting in feels safe, comfortable and relaxed.

> **MYTH:** Dress smart, look the part.
> **FACT:** Don't be uncomfortable in a tight collar you would never normally wear. Over-formal dress is restrictive and will only act as a barrier to your personality.

TRY THIS ...

Ask yourself the following question:

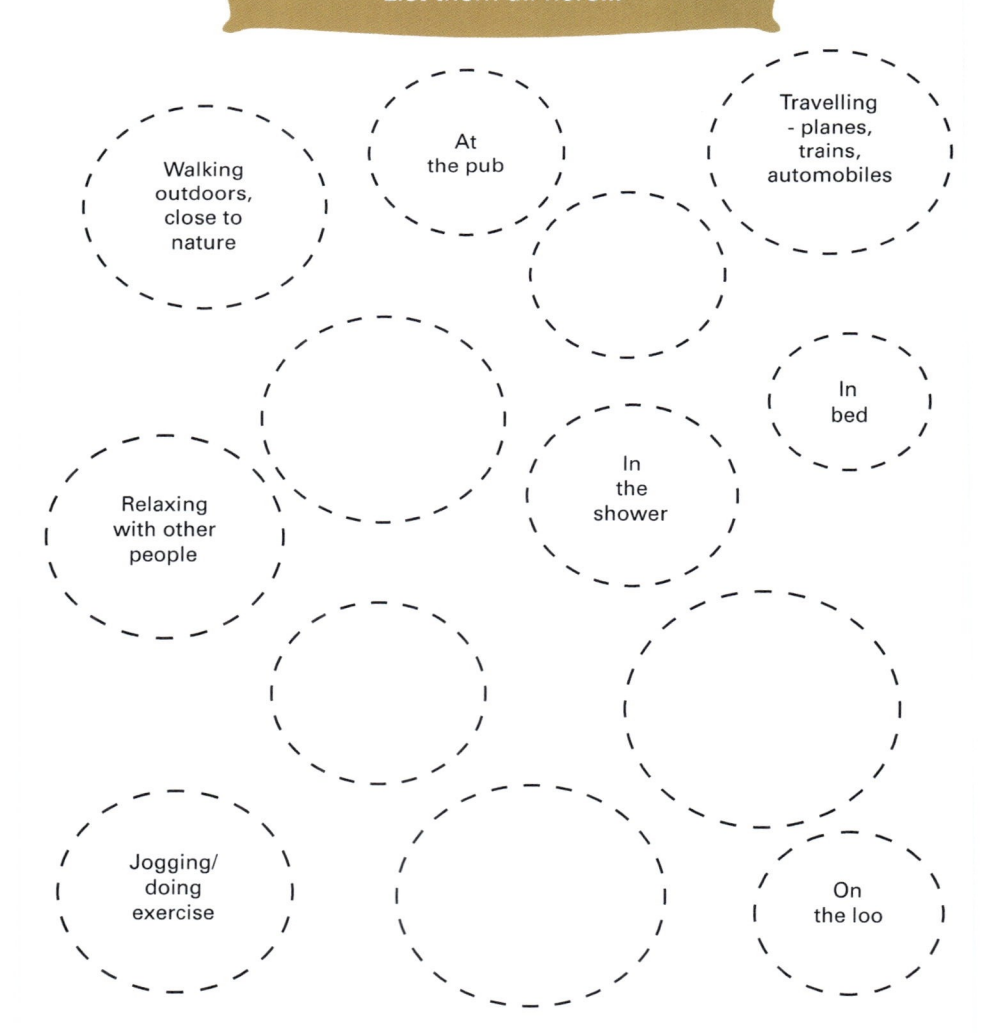

WHERE AM I OR WHAT AM I DOING WHEN I HAVE MY BEST IDEAS/ CLARITY OF THOUGHT?

List them all here...

Walking outdoors, close to nature

At the pub

Travelling - planes, trains, automobiles

In bed

Relaxing with other people

In the shower

Jogging/ doing exercise

On the loo

The Door

It's no accident: people don't do their best thinking in stressful meetings, or when at their desks. It's all to do with the two types of processing power and how you are able to access them.

What dictates your access to each part of your brain's power is a connecting... well, it's hard to explain, let's call it a door (scientists call it the Reticular Activating System). The amount of open or closed-ness of this door will dictate what parts of your brain you have access to at any given time, and the door opens and closes in direct response to your environment and emotional state.

The reticular activating system (RAS), or extrathalamic control modulatory system, is a set of connected nuclei in the brains of vertebrates that is responsible for regulating arousal and sleep-wake transitions. The RAS is the portal through which nearly all information enters the brain (smells are the exception; they go directly into your brain's emotional area.) The RAS filters the incoming information and affects what you pay attention to, how focused you are, and what is not going to get access to all three pounds of your brain.

(from dummies.com)

There is a sweet spot which occurs around all the occasions that get listed in response to our question above. When you have a clear point of focus, feel safe and relaxed, have clarity of objectives and are comfortable in the moment: that's the sweet spot. We call it being in Flow. In these moments you have predominantly Alpha wave activity in your brain, the doorway is slightly open and both parts of the brain are 'on'. Information can flow between the two, so rather than being limited to seven things, you've got access to the infinite Gb device as well.

So what?

Being in Flow is all about options. In Flow you're best able to make new connections and see things differently. Both when you're preparing and planning your session, and when running a session, being in Flow will mean you'll remember all you have to say, you'll be more aware of what's going on in the room, you'll process things faster and always have choices.

Sounds good, what's the issue then, if Flow comes so easily?

Unfortunately, at work or in pressured situations (hello audience of 150 people!), your default is to have predominantly Beta wave activity: operating on conscious brain alone. Beta is a survival state in which your brain has learned not to get distracted by the subconscious. To achieve this the door (RAS) is shut. You have capacity in your brain for seven bits of data in any given moment. These may or may not include what you were going to say, or where you stored that video on your laptop (the really important one you wanted to show everyone but just can't for the life of you remember which folder you put it in...).

Most of all, your limited capacity means you have no ability to flex and respond to changing circumstances, so when things don't go exactly to plan (and even sometimes when they do) you have no resources to deal with them. You become wedded to a predesigned outcome and journey, and the stammering, sweating and shouting/desire to run away begins.

This is true not just of you leading the session, but also of everyone participating, as they all have brains in their heads too. So, throughout the rest of this book, the content is designed to help get you and your participants into Flow – it's a book full of Flow tips.

MYTH: Notes-free is the dream delivery method.

FACT: Who can memorise and learn everything they're going to say for every interaction they're going to have. Make it easy – use notes! Having a written plan helps you relax and then you can focus on the delivery, not worrying about what's coming next.

TRY THIS ...

Knowing what gets you into Flow state (see previous exercise), can you take some of those principles and apply them to your working environment in a way that's appropriate for your particular context (if group showers work for you all, be our guest!)?

To get you started, here are some of our favourites that, even in the most conservative of workplaces or teams, you should be able to take advantage of.

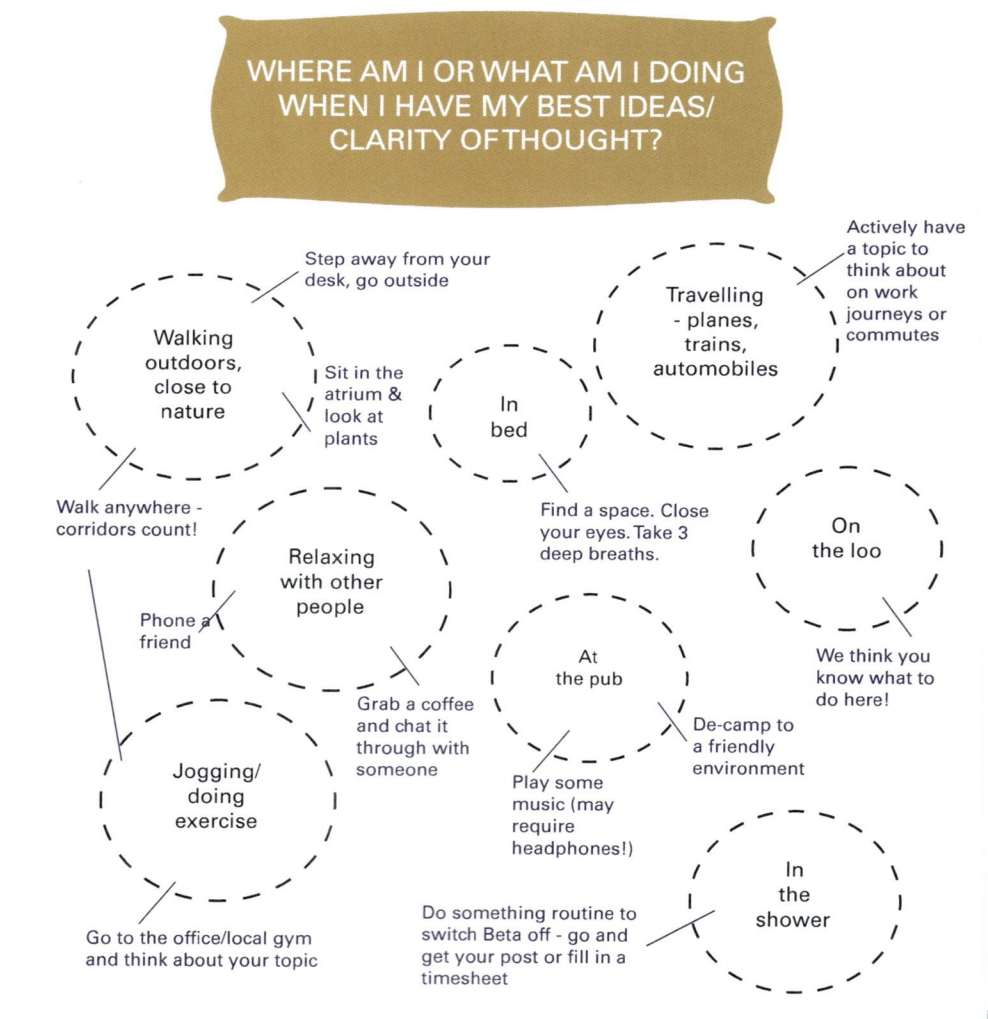

YOUR INNER JAZZ MONKEY

MYTH: Everything needs to be perfect, mistakes are a disaster.

FACT: Only you noticed the spelling mistake on slide 33. It's just not a big deal. They don't know what they don't know. If they've never experienced this before, they don't know how it should be. Rather than throwing out the baby with the bathwater, just smooth over it and carry on.

There's one thing we do agree with the other presentation books about. The pressure people put on themselves to give great presentations and lead great sessions really exists. However, we don't believe the root cause is always a fear of speaking in public. Every human being has spoken in public successfully before. There must be more going on. And there is.

The real demon is the one that won't allow you to be in the moment. The one that demands unreasonable levels of precision and dinner-party style jokes from yourself, the voice that tells you your career depends on this and you can control it all if you try hard enough.

The irony is that the more you try to control things, the more Beta activity will go on in your brain, and the less options you will have, therefore the more likely the bad things are to come true. What will help you more than planning a funny quip or get-out for every clever question, is to learn to let go, and be relaxed in the moment. Or as we call it, to release your inner jazz monkey.

Jazz Monkey *(noun)*: An inner being or spirit, which allows one to make light of difficulty and improvise in the face of change while playing within a clear structure and delivering an agreed output.

Jazz Monkey *(verb)*: To create the appropriate energy and vibe for yourself and others to get things done efficiently and enjoyably.

Everyone's Jazz Monkey is different. This is about being your best self, not about adopting the personality and characteristics of other people (that's Dark Donkey. Read other books for that).

Your Jazz Monkey comes out in full force when you are in Flow.

So let's dig a bit deeper into Flow...

THE ELEMENTS OF FLOW

All too often in life, when asked "How are you?" the knee-jerk reaction is "I'm fine". It's an involuntary shield we use to protect our daily selves from the depths of what's really going on for us – and it's the socially acceptable way to move a conversation on, and avoid difficult personal topics in a social or business context.

And that is, well, fine. But. When checking in with ourselves we need to go a bit deeper. Self-describing as 'fine' doesn't cut it when it comes to allowing your Jazz Monkey to run free and you to be in full Flow. We need a way to diagnose how we REALLY are, that enables us to do something about it, if we want to be able to turn on the monkey in situations where we'd previously find that difficult.

In other words, we need some words to help us get beneath the 'fine' and into how we're really doing in any given moment. So let's get into the elements of Flow.

TRY THIS ...

1. Find a device that can play music – your phone, a laptop, or a good old fashioned record player would all do the job – and a space where you can listen to it uninterrupted.

   NOTE: This exercise works best if the pieces of music are random and unknown to you, so you could get someone else to choose them for you.

   If you have no friends nearby, you can always use our Flow Exercise playlist on Spotify (search for The Business Speakeasy – and for legal reasons please note, other music sources are available!)

2. Select a track and listen to it for about 60 seconds, while making some notes here about how the music makes you feel.

NOTES:

3. Do the same with a second track – select, and listen to it for about 60 seconds, while making some notes here about how this piece makes you feel.

> **NOTES:**

4. Now look back at the way both pieces of music made you feel. Are they the same, or different? What kind of things did you notice?

> **NOTES:**

WHAT IS FLOW THEN?

Your Flow is composed of different elements, each of which have an individual impact on how you are in any given moment.

Let's take a stroll through the forest of Flow and pause a while by the stream of being (sounds slightly wrong, doesn't it – but it made us laugh…), and look at the impact each element can have.

PHYSICAL:

What's going on in and around your body

Are you sitting comfortably? Are you tired? Hungry or well fed? Wearing clothes that aren't distracting you? Too hot, too cold or just right?

In business, we often ignore our physical selves. We live up in our heads, and even when our bodies are screaming at us to eat, go to the loo or stand up and stretch, we plough on with the business at hand. If you want proof of this for yourself, just suggest stopping for a loo and coffee break about 90 minutes in to a 3 hour meeting and see the relief on everyone else's face!

The thing is, when your physical self is not comfortable, the distraction sucks energy and prevents you from concentrating on anything else. So even if you think you are managing to successfully strategise whilst your tummy rumbles, it's taking a large proportion of brain power just to resist heading straight for the canteen or the nearest sandwich shop.

So how can you get proactive about managing your physicality? There are lots of things you can do to help your poor body to stay comfy during business interactions – but unfortunately most people are so busy tweaking their slides at the last minute that they forget about looking after these basic elements of Flow. Here are some starter-for-ten suggestions from us:

- Get a good sleep – the night before a big presentation it can be tempting to stay up worrying and practicing. Don't! The less sleep you get, the harder your brain will have to work the next day.

- Make sure you're not going to get hungry – eat before the meeting or bring snacks with you

- Have a bottle of water so you're not left dry-mouthed and parched at a critical moment

- Select an outfit that's comfy and that you know you'll feel good in (now is not the time to try out those new skyscraper heels or super-skinny low-cut trousers!)

- Have layers so you can shed or add them in response to the room temperature, or better still, take control of the thermostat and make yourself comfortable!!!

- Go to the loo! Make sure you have time for it and then don't forget to do it.

- Manage the caffeine – for sure, have a coffee but perhaps not ten or twelve.

There's a ton more where the above came from, but you get the idea! Start to tune in to your physical needs and take action to prevent them becoming urgent or distracting, and your brain will thank you for it.

INTELLECTUAL:

The thinking and processing going on in your head

We're clever, us humans. We process every reaction we are conscious of, usually in self-conversation (or by making pictures in our heads). This is an amazing feat, but it can mean that our brains are working non-

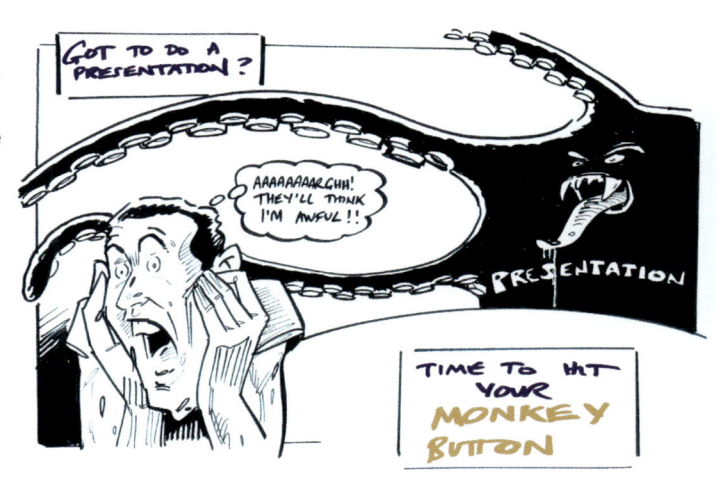

stop while we are awake – understanding, evaluating, extrapolating, deducing, disaster-planning, creating, ideating, analysing, worrying... it gets pretty busy in there!

When we are triggered by someone or something, human intellectual processing has only a few core patterns. You know yourself best so we'll leave it up to you to decide which animal you tend to become under pressure:

- The hectic spaniel – busy, busy, busy, running here and there getting snippets and teasers of a bigger picture but constantly being distracted onto new topics. Rushing from one thing to the next at what feels like a hundred miles an hour, never quite able to finish any one train of... SQUIRREL!

- The fixated lemming – there's one set of thoughts going on, and however much you might want to change the subject, your brain is ruthlessly pursuing that direction. Going on and on and on about the same topic, it's driving you mad but you're swept along in the wave of singular focus even though you know it's going to take you over a cliff at some point.

- The head-in-the-sand ostrich – it's all happening around you, things are kicking off, but you've disconnected from that and all you are focussing on is your plan and sticking to it. Your brain does not want to deal with the issues, you're ready to sit and wait it out while pretending everything is OK.

- The startled rabbit - although usually a highly capable and articulate individual, your mind suddenly goes blank. Your brain freezes. It feels like you have nothing to say and every moment drags on into an eternity. Grasping desperately inside your suddenly-empty skull for something to say, you feel your eyes get wide and your mouth turn into the Sahara – and there's still nothing.

In order to get yourself in the owl-like intellectual space, you may need to clear away some stuff that triggers the intellectual heebie jeebies, in advance of a session. This could mean that you:

- Speak to stakeholders to find out their views, rather than wondering and trying to read their facial expressions (by the way, never rely on this, many people have the most awful listening faces and you can get a completely wrong impression about what they are thinking!)

- Go for a walk to clear your head of the issues that were discussed in your previous meeting

- Make yourself a cheat sheet that you can review just before the meeting, to make sure you have all the key info top of mind

- Get into the room a bit early so you can make sure you have all the equipment you're going to need to hand – and check that your video works on the meeting room laptop.

Basically, we're saying, if you want a clear head, take the time upfront to clear it!

EMOTIONAL:

The feelings you're experiencing

No matter how hard we try to control them, our feelings seem to occur independent of need or appropriateness. The truth is, emotions are chemical, and act at a cellular, microscopic level in our bodies, and therefore controlling them in the moment is a difficult brief.

Often we confuse emotional and intellectual activity, so let's get clear. Emotion is not rational or logical. Emotion rarely speaks to us in conversational tones inside our head – it drives the intellect to tell us things instead. When we say emotions we're referring to feelings you experience, that can be labelled with words like happy, sad, frustrated, elated, frightened, angry, nervous, confident.

Everyone experiences these feelings differently, and for many of us, emotions are deeply tied to certain circumstances, experiences or situations – and so can be awakened by something happening that reminds us of a previous occasion.

So what can you do to ensure you are emotionally positive, which will enable you to be in Flow when you need to? Well, that's going to be very personal – but we'd suggest it involves reminding yourself of previous experiences which have been positive, and situations in which you have felt great, or confident, or excited (whatever feeling you need to have in the upcoming situation) before.

Tactics we have seen people use successfully (and used ourselves) include:

- Sitting quietly and doing a visualisation of a previous presentation that went well in the past, and bringing to mind how that felt
- Listening to a certain piece of music
- Looking at particular photos
- Reading a message from someone giving you positive feedback
- Watching videos that make you laugh

Whatever you choose, prime yourself with positive emotions in advance, so you can get into Flow more readily.

RELATIONAL:

The connection you have to other people

No person is an island. We all exist at the heart of a complex web of relationships that travel through the world with us and make us who we are. Our relationships, with family, friends, acquaintances and co-workers have a deep and profound influence on our ability to achieve Flow state.

A lack of ability to achieve Flow may be due to a relational issue within the room – a disturbance in the force between the people gathered together. It may equally be due to an issue in a relationship you have with someone outside the room.

Fancy trying to give a sales pitch for your company's latest yogurt launch immediately after a shouty, accusatory phone call with a close friend or family member? No, nor do we.

So what can you do to resolve or manage relational issues so that they don't obstruct your Flow? That depends. If there's an issue within a group of colleagues, perhaps you need to get them together in advance of a big workshop or meeting, and have them discuss the problem before getting into your update on the half-year sales forecast. If, however, it's a personal relationship issue, you may need to recognise that being in the meeting is not going to help you resolve it, and ask your brain to let it go for a short while to allow you to be fully present in whatever is happening right now.

You can also take advantage of positive relationships to help boost your Flow. Try:

- Making a photo album of favourite moments with your favourite people to flick through in advance of a big presentations

- Planning in a phone call with a loved-one a few minutes before your big moment, so they can tell you how loved and amazing you are (do warn them you're going to do this though, as a conversation about whether you can pick up something for supper just doesn't have the same level of impact)

- Arriving early at the meeting you'll be presenting in so that you can chat to a few people, thus turning an audience of strangers into a set of new friends

SPIRITUAL:

Your sense of purpose around the situation

We're not talking religion here (but if that's what floats your boat, tap into it!) – rather we're talking about your general sense of purpose and belief.

A positive spiritual state involves being certain that *here is where I need to be right now*, believing that *I am the best person to be doing this*. Agreeing that *the team I am with are the right team for the job*, or *the audience I'm speaking to are the people who need to hear me*.

Often people feel a lack of spiritual purpose in situations where they feel 'done to' - perhaps because you were not the first choice person to do a particular task, or you've been cornered into doing something unwillingly. Perhaps you feel it's a bit unfair that you should be the one on the spot this time, or the other activities you could be doing seem much more worthwhile to you.

Getting a positive spiritual vibe going usually involves being a little more personal than we are used to in a business setting. It means spending some time thinking about the "why" of a particular situation, and working out why now, why you, why the rest of the people involved, and examining your expectations and beliefs around it.

This might mean being somewhat selfish – though you can keep the selfishness private! Perhaps doing your sixth repetition on the fire and safety induction in 3 months is not particularly exciting for you – but can you find a reason to make it so?

Try asking "What's in it for me?", or if you want to be more generous, "Why is this important in the world?".

Laddering up to the fact that it's a chance to try out a new approach to presenting without PowerPoint, or that your words could save someone's life someday, is usually helpful in finding a spiritual driver.

Leaving this sense of purpose to chance is not an option. If you leave a lack of spiritual Flow hanging, it disrupts everything else. It undermines your feelings, gets you niggling and worrying, interferes with relationships and can even make you feel physically unwell.

So don't ignore this essential element. Take time to find your spiritual 'buy in' to any given situation, and bring it to mind before starting, so your North Star is well and truly in place when it's most important.

The importance of the concept of Flow is not to be in 100% active Flow state at all times. Nobody can manage that - it's energy hungry and you'd be exhausted! It is, however, about consciously tuning in to things you can do to get yourself in the best possible place when you need to, for example when you're standing at the front of a room with eyes on you.

Finally, let's be clear. Being in Flow is not about pretending other things are not going on, and ignoring problems that are relevant in life right now. It is about recognising that those things exist, and taking a decision to deal with them outside of the presentation or meeting you're in, if they aren't directly related. It's leaving your baggage at the door to enable you to be fully present, in Flow, for this interaction that's happening right now.

MYTH: It doesn't matter what you wear.
FACT: Human beings make judgements based on their first visual impressions. Wear something that you feel makes you look GOOD. It's not the clothes themselves, but the way you'll hold yourself in clothes you feel good about, that will make the difference.

TRY THIS ...

Either knowing what you know about yourself, or with input from a few of the people who know you best, fill in your jazz monkey map (see next pages).

This will help you to find out what your genuine monkey looks like - remember, everybody's is different and we want you to be yourself.

Go beneath the surface - beyond the obvious words like 'positive' and 'good'. The more specific you can be, the better, because these specifics can be built on to create a great set of Jazz Monkey Flow tactics that are personal to you.

First, bring to mind a situation in which you were not quite communicating or feeling at your best. Ideally, this is a work situation, and one which is not highly emotionally charged. You need to be happy to revisit and learn from the situation, so don't upset yourself! Fill in the "Not in Flow" template over the page for this situation

Then, bring to mind a situation in which you were communicating and feeling at your best, and fill in the "In Flow" template on the next page for this situation.

TRY THIS ...

The Situation

What were you doing? Who was there? Where was it etc.?

I struggled to release my Jazz Monkey because/when...

Your Flow

What was going on for you (Physically, Intellectually, Emotionally, Relationally, Spiritually)?

Things that made me feel less relaxed

People present/environment you were in/ physical space/music etc.

The Situation

What were you doing? Who was there? Where was it etc.?

I knew I'd released my Jazz Monkey because/when...

Your Flow

What was going on for you (Physically, Intellectually, Emotionally, Relationally, Spiritually)?

Things that made me feel more relaxed

People present/environment you were in/ physical space/music etc.

Now we need to spot some themes. Look at the stimulus you've just created in your Flow Maps, and start to pull out what kind of stuff helps you be at your best, for example:

- Which type of people help you out?
- What type of physical space are you best in? Do you like pictures and music?
- Do you feel best when you are still or when you are moving?
- Does sitting quietly or going for a walk help you more?

Here's some space for you to note down some themes – use it as you wish...

Now it's time to plan some tactics – using the themes from the previous page and your Alpha State Triggers from the earlier exercise. Start with your top 3 and fill them in here. Don't forget to think about any supporting structures or materials that will help – for example, if your tactic is to play funky music, your structure may be to build yourself a jazz monkey playlist.

My top 3 Jazz Monkey release tactics are:

TACTIC

SUPPORTING STRUCTURES (IF REQ'D)

1.

2.

3.

Our hi-tech tip: take a photo of this page on your phone so it's always with you (no, we don't have an app!!!)

DIALS

Discovering your dials

The more you can understand about your Flow and what gets you there, the more choice you have about what happens next. Removing the distractions created by things that are not quite right, frees up brain space and bandwidth to process and be brilliant in the moment. And that gives you the chance to play with your delivery Dials.

Everyone, even the most monotone of people, has expressive range. We use it all the time in casual conversation, but in more formal presentation situations it can be something we tone down, either by choice or through nerves.

This range is what makes you interesting to watch and listen to. Your Dials plus your Superpowers mean you are unique and that nobody else will deliver the same materials in quite the same way you do. Hooray for that! So spend some time exploring your Dials.

Did you know that in human communication, only 7% of the meaning is transmitted through the words. 7 per cent! No wonder we can get in so much trouble with an email! The remaining meaning comes from tone of voice (38%) and body language (55%).

This means that the more you vary your tone and movement, the greater an impact your communication will have - so let's get you using those Dials!

MYTH: You've got the graveyard slot.

FACT: You get the energy you create in a group. It doesn't matter the time of day except to help you work out how much needs to be done to create the right energy for what you need to do.

A great way to play with Dials is to find a friend and have a chat as usual, while having fun with your expressive range under each of the dials below. Pick a new score on one of the dials for each sentence you say and see what happens.

(If you've forgotten all your words, and are struggling for a sentence to say, try repeating this one with different dial settings: "My Monkey has the day off on Tuesdays, so would you mind tying your own shoelaces?")

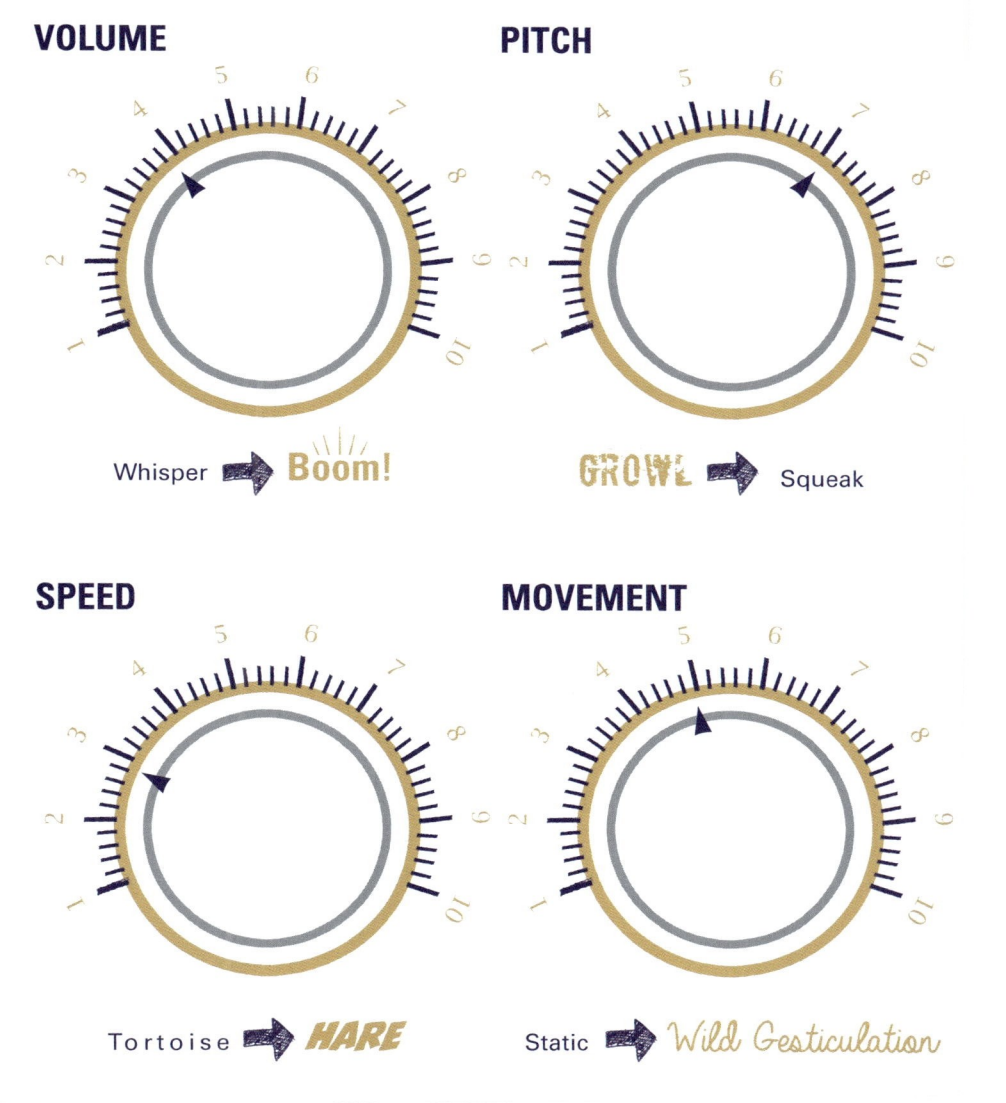

VOLUME

Whisper ➡ **Boom!**

PITCH

GROWL ➡ Squeak

SPEED

Tortoise ➡ *HARE*

MOVEMENT

Static ➡ *Wild Gesticulation*

-4-

BRINGING
CONTENT
TO LIFE

TELLING COMPELLING STORIES

It's no accident that we find it easy to remember a well-crafted story. Think you don't remember them well? How many times have you had to take a pen and paper to the cinema in order to make notes?

There's a ton of research that demonstrates how the human brain has evolved to learn through story. You can go and read up on all of this in your own time, but for now let's just say that a story is a great way to deliver information through a secret passage directly into the Subconscious brain, without having to get past the Conscious, rational gate-keeper.

So, if you want to communicate in a way that makes an impact, stories will be your friend.

For those of you reading this and starting to panic - because you deal in pie charts and statistics, or because you're not a raconteur - calm down! Stories can be very simple structures, that anyone can tell, if you follow our simple structure.

We're simple folk, and so after reading and studying all the high-brow thinking on constructing great stories, we've identified the 5 parts to any great story arc.

Use this structure to shape your story and we promise it will hang together and convince your audience.

THE STORY ARC

The Point: Why are you telling the story? What is the take-away message?

Don't hold this back until the end. When people know the theme of the story upfront, their brains pick up on all the corroborating details that confirm the message as the story proceeds.

Top tips: Use phrases like "This is a story about…", "The point of this story is…"

The Hero: Who or what is the story about?

Every story needs a hero to focus around. The hero can be a person, a thing, a process, even a team. The most important aspect of the hero is that audience can empathise with them/it, so spend a little time bringing them to life in a way that makes them likeable..

Top tips: Try not to make yourself the all-singing, all-dancing hero, because nobody likes a show-off! If the story is about you, perhaps tell it about an imaginary third person and reveal the truth later, or be self-deprecating to ensure your listeners are still connecting to you.

The Challenge: What was the hero up against? Was there any jeopardy? What needed to be overcome/stopped/prevented or achieved?

If your story were a movie, the Challenge would be the bit before we know it's all going to be alright. Think Luke seeing the Death Star for the first time from his X-Wing, Harry facing Voldemort even though he's never managed to summon a successful patronus, or Thanus with a fist full of infinity stones.

The A-ha: How was the Challenge resolved?

This is the moment in the story where our brains are satisfied. It's like the punchline of a joke so make sure it's linked to the Challenge and the Point.

Top tips: if you are communicating about an issue that is still a Challenge, then a story is a brilliant way to do it - just use this moment to bring in the possible/future A-ha that will resolve things, then watch people sign up to help you deliver it.

The Impact: What happened as a result?

Here you stitch everything together, and put a bow on it so that human brains can package your message away neatly. If it helps, repeat the Point to emphasise how the Impact justifies it.

Top Tips: Make sure you go beyond business outcomes and express some of the human benefits too, as human brains often don't relate to "3 percent increase in market share" as much as they do to "and the Brand Manager was promoted". Express the impact from multiple perspectives to make sure you catch the interest of everyone in the room.

Any story can have an infinite number of variations - often elements fit under several headings so we'd suggest mapping it out in bullet point or keyword form first before going long-hand, and find out which combination feels comfortable to you and brings the Point alive.

An added benefit of this structure is that it makes data-heavy information much easier to remember, because your own human brain finds it more memorable too!

TRY THIS ...

Guess the Movie - can you identify the movie from the story below?

 This story illustrates that people can overcome seemingly insurmountable odds by working together.

 Meet Mikey, and his gang of misfits - a rabble of kids living on a quiet estate in smalltown America. They're good kids, who want nothing more than to hang out together and have fun on their bikes.

 Their town is under threat though, from developers who want to annex the land in order to build a golf course for the nearby country club. This means they'd need to split up and move away to new homes. but there's nothing they can do about it - the residents just don't have the money to buy the developers out.

 While packing up their homes, one day the kids end up in an attic and discover a gold coin and a map, believed to lead to a pirate's treasure horde that has never been found. Banding together for what might be their last adventure, they each use their individual talents to overcome a series of obstacles on a journey through underground caves and booby traps, and to outwit the local criminals who are also on the trail of the treasure.

 The horde of gold is bigger than anyone imagined, and the kids claim it as their own. They buy out the developers, save the homes of the whole community, and prevent their gang from having to separate - all because they worked together and achieved the seemingly impossible.

To practise using the Storytelling Tool, try playing Guess the Movie with some friends - taking turns to describe a movie plot using the 5 parts we've suggested.

> **MYTH:** There is a formula to follow that will guarantee you success.
> **FACT:** Every situation is different, you're going to need to apply a bit of brain power and creativity to get the most from what this book has to teach. But there are some big principles you can use to guide you in any situation.

> **MYTH:** It's got to last an hour.
> **FACT:** The longest you can 'present' to someone for, and have their full attention is 10 minutes. Well, seven. Definitely 5 anyway. The point is, they need to speak too in order to stay actively engaged. Make it a conversation!

Answer: The Goonies - if you haven't seen it, it's a classic, drop everything and watch it now!

GOING MULTI-SENSORY

Have you ever had any of the following experiences at work:

1. Come out of a presentation feeling as though you have been reading a document from the screen?

2. Found your attention wandering from a person who is sharing facts, despite being interested in the subject matter?

3. Been shown a picture by an excited colleague, but failed to be excited by it yourself?

As humans, we have five senses but many of us prefer to experience the world through one or two of them - and this is also how we communicate with others. In business this becomes even more exaggerated, with a universal default to wordy PowerPoint slides, emails and white paper-style documents. It's enough to leave anyone desperate for a box-set of an evening, just to help top up our visual quota.

The good news is, it's easy to keep everyone's attention and get your point across if you make sure you're transmitting to (and with) the 3 main communication styles.

Let's take sharing a new budget plan as an example - here are some ways to make it multi-sensory! Your only limitation is your imagination.

Using images, shapes, diagrams and colours.

Get out of PowerPoint! Represent the budget in a 3D way: use a series of test tubes filled to different levels with coloured water, Lego bricks stuck together or even pieces of different sized and coloured paper arranged on a wall.

Using words, facts, lists and data.

Give people the key details, highlight the important numbers and describe their contribution to the overall plan.

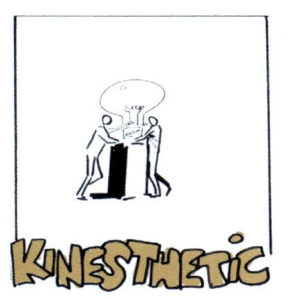

Using stories, emotions, movement and experiences.

Give the team a set of monopoly money and get them to 'spend it' as per the plan, or leave the profit number off your spreadsheet and ask them to work it out.

Remember, you will have a style you prefer and find most engaging. Don't discount the others just because they don't appeal to you. Planning to communicate using all 3 styles at every opportunity means you'll be engaging your whole audience every time.

-5-

HANDLING YOUR AUDIENCE

> **MYTH:** Meetings involve projectors + darkened rooms + boardroom tables/loads of chairs in rows.
>
> **FACT:** Nobody decorates their home like this. If humans were comfortable engaging with one another in these environments, pubs would look like boardrooms. Forget about what your building facilities manager thinks, and start using the environment like a group of real people.

NAVIGATING YOUR TEAM

(managing your audience, leading the room...)

> **NAVIGATION** *(verb)* – making sure people know what's going on, how they need to behave and what's expected of them in terms of contribution at any given moment during a session.

If people aren't told what's going on, how to behave and what's expected they will make their own decision about what is needed from them. This will be driven by their own context and wishes, and so you'll end up with a lack of alignment and potentially a car crash session.

So it makes sense to get behavioural alignment at the beginning of any interaction. Let the human beings in the room know what you want from them. The doing part is important, but it is the being that will make the biggest difference to the outcome. We call this Navigation.

TRY THIS ...

Think about the meetings you attend regularly. Give them an average score for the effectiveness of the time spent, according to this scale, and mark your score (and a couple of notes on why) on the page here...

Meetings Scoreboard

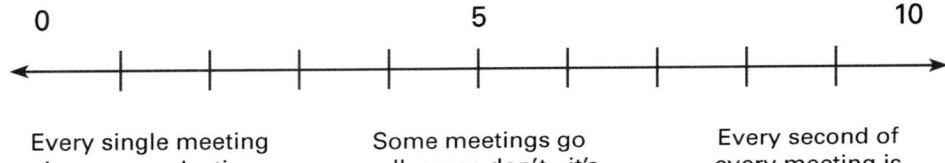

0	5	10

Every single meeting is an unproductive waste of time

Some meetings go well, some don't - it's hard to put my finger on exactly why

Every second of every meeting is productive and time well spent

We've conducted a poll. We've asked thousands of people across lots of cultures and business sectors the same question. The average score in the world of business seems to be 6.

You might be thinking 'that's great – I wish my meetings averaged 6, I only scored 2'. If that's the case, prepare to be amazed by the next section of this book! Or you might, like us, be thinking that an average of 6 is a shame – it means 40% of time in all meetings feels like it's wasted.

The secret is Navigation. Scores of below 5 happen because there isn't any navigation. Scores of 10 don't occur by accident – meetings score 10 out of 10 for effectiveness because deliberate navigation has occurred throughout.

> **DOING** *(verb)* – task-oriented action, the process or agenda followed to get things done.
>
> **BEING** *(verb)* – the beliefs, attitude, energy and passion you bring to the task at hand.

While this might seem obvious, and many people do ask for certain behaviours and share agendas at the start of a session, the ninja level navigator knows that it is a non-stop activity, and that you can never navigate too much.

NORMAL   **NICE!**   **NINJA**

BEHAVIOURAL AGREEMENTS FOR MAXIMUM IMPACT

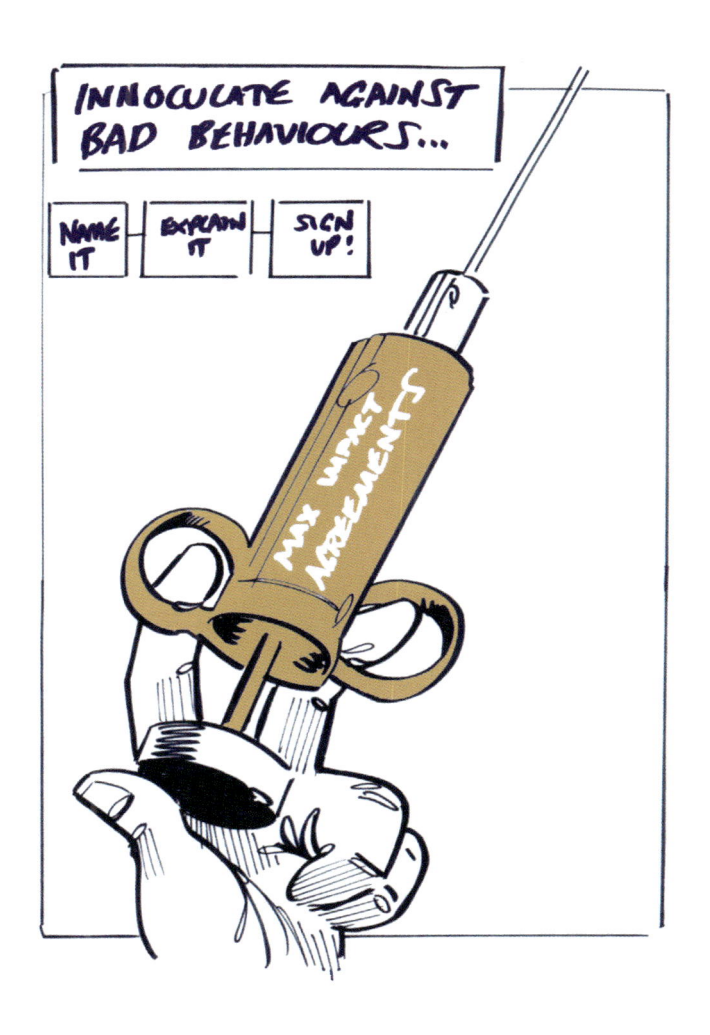

Every engagement needs a behavioural charter. This ensures that everyone involved can be their best, and contribute as much as possible in a way that's useful.

Here are our favourite multi-purpose Maximum Impact agreements to get you started and give you some stimulus to work from, to create your own.

Be fully here

Be in the room physically, spiritually, emotionally and mentally. That means no phones, no laptops, no side conversations, just active listening along with full presence and participation.

Seek the positive

Smart people can easily pick holes in thinking, but super smart people can build on starter thoughts and make them stronger and better. Lean towards new ideas and build them, instead of killing them.

Slow down (to speed up)

It's tempting to want to jump into action and detail, but we're going to spend some time first setting the right energy and getting an agreed focus. This way, we can move through the rest of the content more efficiently knowing all our brains are aligned.

No right no wrong

(A good agreement to use when you need to problem solve or come up with ideas.)

For the moment we are just exploring options. Nobody is correct or incorrect – it's all stimulus. At a later time we will have chance to judge, assess and narrow down.

Let go

Enjoy the ride. We have a plan and we know where you are going, so relax on the journey. The outcome will be better as we'll all be able to access our whole brains.

(A good question to ask here is: has anyone here come along determined to have a bad time and make it an awful session for everyone else? Nobody will say yes! You can remind them of this fact later.)

Own the behavioural context (no-one else will)

It doesn't matter what level of experience, knowledge or understanding you have in the room, all situations involving human beings require the same level of constant navigation. It's this principle that's behind the success of every session we run – and when things go wrong, it's always because we haven't navigated enough.

Navigation is down to you. Don't wait for someone else to do it; in our experience it won't happen. Try tuning in at future meetings and spot the lack of navigation, and start thinking 'if I was running this, what would I do differently?' Having your own opinion and style is vital when it comes to navigating others successfully.

An example of when this might be useful is in combatting issues like 'phone creep' - even when other attendees are all being good about staying focussed and off their phones, one person checks theirs in front of the rest of you. Before you know it, everyone has their phone stuck to their ear and nobody is present in the meeting. This often happens during short breaks. Having a clear agreement to refer back to (and ideally some kind of semaphore shorthand to remind people of the agreement while they're still in conversation) will make it much easier to challenge them without making it into a big deal.

Even better, have a plan before you run your own interactions. Think about the navigation needs of the occasion and the human beings, and plan to navigate accordingly. To get you started, here's your Navigation Checklist. To be used before any/every interaction with human being (or beings) – we've included 3 copies, feel free to scan and make more for yourself.

THE NAVIGATOR'S GEARBOX

We've come across lots of questionnaires and books about leadership styles and facilitation modes, that suggest you need to find the one that works for you. In our experience the best navigators are flexible in the moment and know there's more than one way to respond. There are always options.

Leading a session is a bit like driving – you need to select the right gear for the right moment and be able to shift quickly to adapt to the changes in the road.

You wouldn't carry on driving at 70mph in top gear, if a load of pot holes suddenly appeared, or if the road was twisty and unfamiliar. So don't rely on only one style in leading sessions. Too many facilitators rely on a schoolma'am-like forward style when others could be more useful – the trick is to flex.

We've found 5 gears that can be useful in any situation – and while every situation can be tackled by using any of these navigation gears, some are much more suited to certain situations than others.

The point is not to get hung up on what gear you are in, it's to know you have options. You can therefore effectively switch the way you're managing things to make them even better.

Things to know about the Gearbox:

- The language you use is the biggest indicator of the gear you are using.

- You are always in control and leading the situation – even if you are using Behind.

- Many people have preferred gears, this does not make them more or less effective as navigators, as long as they know how to flex when the situation needs it.

- The last 2 gears are hugely under-rated and often not used. They are likely to become your best friends.

Forward – prescriptive, saying what you want people to do, what is going to happen next and how. People then do it.

Use this gear when: you need to be unambiguous: e.g. you're starting a session, setting up expectations, giving instructions, briefing in activities or discussions, or where you need to close a discussion down and move on.

Beware: the Dictator barking instructions from the room, blindly marching on regardless of the readiness of the group.

Key phrases:

- *"It's going to work like this..."*

- *"We are going to..."*

- *"Here's what's going to happen..."*

- *"Please can you...."*

- *"Team A will..."*

- *"We're going to hear all the views, person A will you please start"*

- *"You've got two minutes to present your case"*

Alongside – collaborative, including people in the decisions about what happens next. People then help you make it happen.

Use this gear when: you genuinely want to create some input from the team and actively participate in the discussion yourself: e.g. you're coming up with solutions in the moment; the group needs to make a choice about the direction things go next.

Beware: getting too involved in the discussion and losing your navigator role; seeking input when you're going to ignore it – you might as well just stay forward in this case.

Key phrases:

- *"I think... what do you think?"*

- *"What options can you see right now - let's list them out"*

- *"There are two things we could tackle now, which would you like to get into first?"*

- *"Let's split into small groups, think about it separately then come back and compare notes"*

Behind – coaching, eliciting people's views about a topic without sharing your own. People express themselves unhindered.

Use this gear when: your views are less important than the group's; you need to create safety and comfort for revealing hidden agendas or cynical views; you genuinely don't know what needs to happen next and you need to understand more about people's state of mind; you want the group to make their own decisions/take the time they need to feel comfortable.

Beware: tuning out of a discussion you should be moderating and missing the need to shift gear and move things on; going behind too early without first having used forward to reassure and explain procedures.

Key phrases:

- *"Tell me what you think about…"*

- *"What would you like to do next?"*

- *"What do you need from me to move things forwards?"*

- *"How are you feeling?"*

- *"Is everyone OK to move on?"*

- *"I'm going to ask for an input from everyone – chip in as the mood takes you"*

- *"What would you like me to cover next?"*

Neutral – creating space for you, the navigator, to respond to changes and check in with what needs to happen next. People are busy by themselves, they don't need you.

Use this gear when: something crops up that you don't immediately know how to handle; you need a break or the opportunity to breathe; you think the group need a break or a change of energy.

Beware: group members worrying that an issue is not going to get dealt with because you haven't tackled it straight away; not giving yourself enough space to do what is required.

Key phrases:

- *"Let's take a 10 minute break then come back and pick up where we left off."*

- *"Let's get all your views on that – have a chat to your neighbor and write down the top 3 issues – you've got 5 minutes"*

- *"Go for a walk and a talk in small groups, and come back with a view on... see you in 15 minutes for a sharing session."*

Park – **pausing; leaving things to settle for a few hours or days then returning to the discussion with fresh minds or additional input.**

Use this gear when: there is insufficient information in the room to enable forward progress; there's a side issue that needs to be tackled but now is not the moment; you or the group are getting tired; there's a big decision to be made and you want everyone to sleep on it before committing; a short coffee break isn't going to give you or the team what they need to move on.

Beware: leaving things hanging without sufficient information on why and what is going to happen next to move things on; being so wedded to your session plan that leave it too long to park the discussion and having to deal with a tired and over-emotional group.

Key phrases:

- *"That's a really good point but it's not core to this meeting – will someone take responsibility to arrange another session to get into it?"*

- *"I think we need to sleep on this before making a decision."*

- *"Let's break for lunch now, and come back to this at the end of the day."*

TRICKY CUSTOMERS

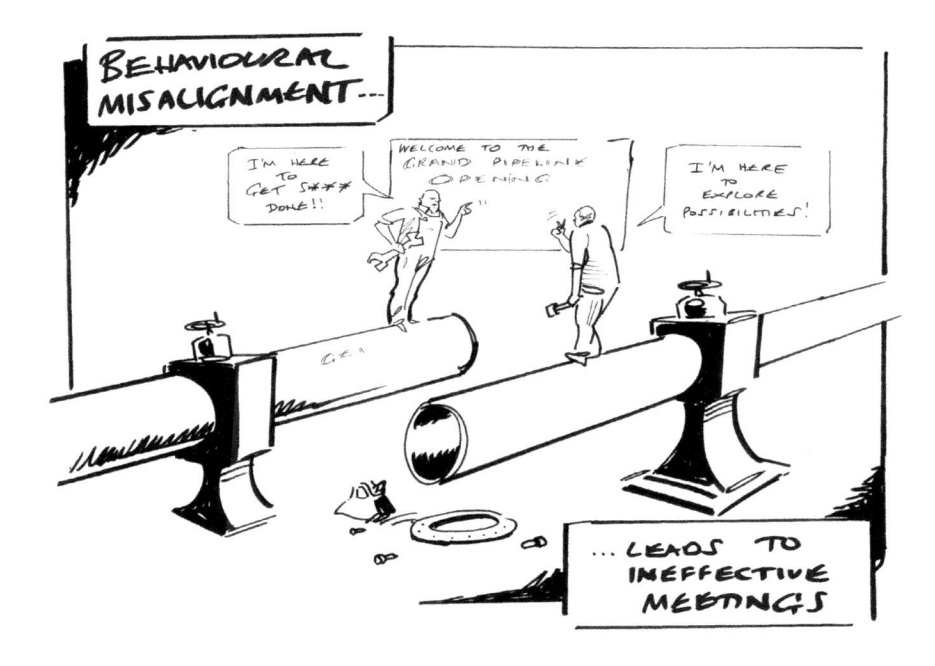

The great news is, the more you tune up to the Navigation that's needed, the more proficient you get at doing it. You'll be able to form your own checklists inside your head, and you'll have a bank of experience to draw on.

The other piece of good news is that Navigation often reduces the bad smell created by those we'll just call "tricky customers" (other names are available and we're sure you've used them at some point).

Just a little bit of Navigation can fill the gaps that allow an awkward, cynical or non-believing colleague to exploit a situation, and cause problems. On the other hand, a lack of clear Navigation creates a lovely muddy swamp of interpretation in which they can roll like joyous hippos, splashing metaphorical mud all over you and everyone else in the room.

So, if you have a known tricky customer, make sure your Navigation takes them into account – from behavioural agreements to clear signposting of when critique will be welcomed and useful, and firm Forward closing down of non-aligned behaviours at other times.

Not only will your sessions be more productive, but your colleagues will love you too: if you're finding this customer tricky, others will be too.

The thing we'd love you to remember is that very rarely does anybody else want to be evil. People only behave they way they do out of desire to help or move things forward in a way they think will be productive. So, if your tricky customer is a particularly special one, our advice would be to spend some one-on-one time with them before any session to understand their perspective and communicate to them what will 'help' the session be a success.

It's easy to leave out this Navigation stuff. It can feel strange asking people for named behaviours, and tackling tricky conversations about personal impact. In the end, it's your choice whether to Navigate or not. Our advice would be – do it, and like the rest of the stimulus in the book, find your own style for it that feels natural and authentic. You won't regret it!

MYTH: They're a difficult audience.
FACT: There's no herd behaviour. Everyone in your group is too busy thinking about their own shit to care that much about making things awkward for you.

-6-

NOT YOUR USUAL PRESENTATION CHECKLIST

Well done, you've made it to the end of our ramble (or perhaps you haven't and you just skipped here, in which case the next piece may not make much sense, don't shoot the messenger!).

On the following pages are some proformas to help you put everything from this book into practice. We've put down some prompting questions in each of the key areas to get you thinking about your presentation and how to make it a success. Of course you're bound to have your own better version of these questions, so feel free to take our stimulus and make your own proforma!

In the meantime, whenever you're planning a presentation or a group session, grab a cuppa and a nice pen, and slow down to speed up with a Not Your Usual Presentation Planning Session – using the proforma on the next pages to get you started. Enjoy!

PRESENTATION: **DATE:**

Communication superpowers: ### Energy, flow and range:

Confidence in your own   Create the right energy
authentic style.   in a room.

More presence and   Tactics to keep you and your
impact in a room.   presentation on track.

- -

What are my existing   Where will the session
Communication Superpowers?   take place?

Could I use opportunity to   When is it happening
develop new Superpowers?   (time of day/month)?

Should I - is it the right forum   What is happening before &
for experimenting?   after it - for me/for others?

- -

**HOW AM I GOING TO MAKE   **WHAT DO I NEED TO PREPARE TO
SURE I AM IN FLOW?**   MAKE BEST USE OF SPACE & ENERGY**

Bringing content to life:

Breathe life into content
(even PowerPoint!)

Tell compelling stories
using a simple structure.

Audience handling:

Get audiences engaged
from the start.

Able to manage
tricky customers.

What inputs do I/
we have?

Who is
in the room?

What outcomes
do we need?

What do they know
at the start?

What points do I/
we want to make?

What is their state of
mind likely to be?

**HOW CAN I USE COMMUNICATION
STYLES? STORIES?**

**WHAT NAVIGATION DO
I NEED TO DO?**

THAT'S ALL FOR NOW...

Being a great communicator isn't a skill you learn, it's a choice you make – the choice to bring the right energy, focus, attitude and behaviours to whatever session you are involved with.

You're a human being, you're born with the ability to get your message across in a passionate and involving way - it's in your DNA, it always has been.

Your colleagues are human too (well most of them!) – with the right navigation not only will they come with you on the journey, they'll enjoy it too and want to come back for more.

There's more than enough time being spent on Business As Usual so take a break once in a while, alphasise your brain and let the Jazz Monkey roam free.

See what it finds.

Love from...

DON'T BE A STRANGER...

We'd love to hear from you with any comments on this book or stories you want to share.

Feel free to contact us, find out more about what we do, or send us champagne, via our website www.thebusinessspeakeasy.com.

Printed in Poland
by Amazon Fulfillment
Poland Sp. z o.o., Wrocław

62336565R00058